Eudora Welty's
WORLD

• *Words on Nature* •

Edited by Patti Carr Black • Watercolors by Robin Whitfield

EDGE PRESS, Jackson, Mississippi

EUDORA WELTY'S WORLD

Words on Nature

By Eudora Welty

Edited by Patti Carr Black

Watercolors by Robin Whitfield

EDGE PRESS

Box 55584

Jackson, Mississippi

edgemiss@aol.com

1-877-949-9935

ISBN: 0-9669782-7-7

Acknowledgments

My deep appreciation to Elizabeth Welty Thompson and Mary Alice Welty White for their interest in this project and their permission to use Eudora Welty's words.

Excerpts from *Losing Battles,* copyright 1970 by Eudora Welty, are used by permission of Random House, Inc.

Excerpts from *The Wide Net and Other Stories,* copyright 1942 and renewed 1970 by Eudora Welty, reprinted by permission of Harcourt, Inc.

Excerpts from *A Curtain of Green and Other Stories,* copyright 1938 and renewed 1966 by Eudora Welty, reprinted by permission of Harcourt, Inc.

Excerpts from *The Golden Apples,* copyright 1947 and renewed 1975 by Eudora Welty, reprinted by permission of Harcourt, Inc.

Excerpts from *Delta Wedding,* copyright 1946, 1945 and renewed 1974, 1973 by Eudora Welty, reprinted by permission of Harcourt, Inc.

Eudora Welty's
WORLD
• Words on Nature •

EUDORA WELTY was deeply attuned to the natural world. As a young woman she enjoyed long walks and country hikes; for thirty years she was an active gardener as her mother's "yard boy;" in later years she relished drives in the countryside; and at the end of her life she was still watching squirrels "spiral down" the oak tree outside her window. Her powers of observation were keen and constantly at work. As a passenger in a car, she could spot a rabbit in a field passing it at sixty-five miles an hour. Welty's knowledge of and pleasure in nature is abundantly apparent in her fiction. These selections are offered not only for their descriptive quality, but for her imaginative and provocative use of words. This small book is for lovers of nature and lovers of language.

Patti Carr Black

The outside world is the vital component to my inner life.... My imagination takes its strength and guides its direction from what I see and hear and learn and feel and remember of my living world.

Eudora Welty

Hickory Tree

TREES

CRAPE MYRTLE

The crape myrtle had a last crown of bloom on top,

once white, now faintly nutmegged. The ground below

was littered with its shed bark, and the limbs shone like

human limbs, lithe and warm, pink.

        — "The Wanderers"

MIMOSA

Fragile, delicate, cloud-like it rose on its pale trunk and
spread its long level arms. His mother pointed to it.
Among the trembling leaves the feathery puffs of sweet
bloom filled the tree like thousands of paradisiacal birds
all alighted at an instant.... It seemed to be the mimosa
tree that lighted the garden, for its brightness and
fragrance overlaid all the rest. Out of its graciousness
this tree suffered their presence and shed its splendor
upon him and his mother.

— "First Love"

MAGNOLIA

Magnolia's the loudest tree there is in a storm,"
said Doc.

— "The Wide Net"

CYPRESS

The cypress trunks four feet thick in the water's edge
stood opened like doors of tents in Biblical engravings.

— *Delta Wedding*

BOIS D'ARC

There was not a breath of air. But all the heart-shaped leaves on the big bois d'arc tree by the house were as continually on the spin as it they were hung on threads. And whirly-winds of dust marched, like scatterbrained people, up and down the farm track, or pegged across the fields, popped off into nowhere.

— *Losing Battles*

LIVE OAKS

…the live oaks—trunks flaky black and white now,

as if soot, not rain, had once fallen from heaven on them,

and the wet eyes of cut-off limbs on them; and the whole

rainlighted spread roof of green leaves that moved like

children's lips in speech, high up.

— "The Wanderers"

SYCAMORES

Along the bank of the river, the sycamore trees in the school yard were tinged on top with yellow, as though acid had been spilled on them from some traveling spoon.

— *Losing Battles*

WILLOWS

The willow trees leaned overhead under muscadine vines,
and their trailing leaves hung like waterfalls in the
morning air. The thing that seemed like silence must
have been the endless cry of all the crickets and locusts
in the world, rising and falling.

— "The Wide Net"

CEDARS

There were leggy cedars still lining the old property,

their trunks white and knobbed like chicken bones.

— "The Wanderers"

Trumpet Vine

FLOWERS

ROSES

Rosebushes thick and solid as little Indian mounds

were set here and there with their perennial,

worn little bird nests like a kind of bloom.

— *Delta Wedding*

DAHLIAS

They brought dahlias with scalded leaves hanging down
their stems like petticoats, darker and heavier
prince's-feathers that looked like a stormy sunset.

— *Losing Battles*

ALTHEA

…the althea bush with its hundreds of flowers
already spindling, like messages already read
and folded up.

— Losing Battles

COSMOS

In the row with them, the cosmos flowers

barely stirring on their stems under the fine soft rain

were washed bright as the embroidery on the pillowcase

Miss Lexie wore over her hat.

— Losing Battles

WISTERIA

The wisteria that grew there with it looked nearly as old as the bell; its trunk was like an old, folded, gray quilt packed up against the post...

— *Losing Battles*

ZINNIA

In the light from the rain, different from sunlight,
everything appeared to gleam unreflecting from
within itself in its quiet arcade of identity. The green
of the small zinnia shoots was very pure, almost burning.
One by one, as the rain reached them, all the individual
little plants shone out, and the branching vines.
The pear tree gave a soft rushing noise, like the wings
of a bird alighting.

— *A Curtain of Green*

CANNAS

Cannas came around the house on either side

in a double row, like the Walls of Jericho, with their

blooms unfurled—Miss Beulah's favorite colors,

the kind that would brook no shadow.

        — *Losing Battles*

CAMELLIAS

The camellia bushes had all set their buds,
choosing the driest and busiest time, and if they
did not get water they would surely drop them,
temperamental as they were.

— *Delta Wedding*

MONTBRETIAS

A hummingbird moved down the last colored thing,

the wall of montbretias as though it were writing on it

in words.

— Losing Battles

SUMAC

Sumac hung over the way ahead, studded with long heads like red-hot pokers.

— *Losing Battles*

HONEYSUCKLE

Here sweet dusty honeysuckle—for the vines were
pinkish-white with dust, like icing decorations on a cake,
each leaf and tendril burdened—perfumed a gentler air,
along with the smell of cut-flower stems that had been
in glass jars since some Sunday, and the old-summer
smell of the big cedars.

— *Delta Wedding*

NIGHT-BLOOMING CEREUS

Virgie looked at the naked, luminous, complicated flower,

large and pale as a face on the dark porch.

— "The Wanderers"

CASTOR BEAN

They were eye to eye with the finger-shaped leaves of
the castor bean plants, put out like those gypsy hands
that part the curtains at the back of rolling wagons, and
wrinkled and coated over like the fortuneteller's face.

— "Moon Lake"

BLACKBERRIES

Dense mounds of blackberry bushes held their own through the sheets of dust, looking like giant iron cooking pots set the width of the home pasture.

— *Losing Battles*

VINES

Vines, a magnificent and steamy green, covered more
and more of the trees, played over them like fountains.

— "Moon Lake"

BOXWOOD

Taking the posts was a hedge that went up from the
landing, higher than anybody's head with tiny leaves
nobody could count—boxwood; it was bitter-green
to smell, the strong fearless fragrance of things
nobody has been to see.

— *Delta Wedding*

Tanager

BIRDS

BIRDS

For a moment nothing broke the silence except a bird
shuffling about in the althea bush like somebody looking
through a bureau drawer where something had been
put away.

— Losing Battles

HUMMINGBIRD

He was a little emerald bobbin, suspended as always
before the opening four o'clocks. Metallic and misty
together, tangible and intangible, splendid and fairy-like,
the haze of his invisible wings mysterious, like the ring
around the moon—had anyone ever tried to catch him?
Not she. Let him be suspended there for a moment
each year for a hundred years— incredibly thirsty,
greedy for every drop in every four-o'clock trumpet
in the yard, as though he had them numbered—
then dart.

— "June Recital"

MOCKINGBIRD

Outside the closed window a mockingbird began to sing.
Clytie held back the curtain and pressed her ear against
the glass. The rain had stopped. The bird's song sounded
in liquid drops down through the pitch-black trees and
the night.

— "Clytie"

CHIMNEY SWIFTS

The chimney swifts ticked in the deepening sky overhead, going round and round, tilting like taut little bows drawn with arrows ready.

— *Losing Battles*

MOURNING DOVE

The mourning dove called his three notes,

kept its short silence—which was its mourning?—-

and called three more.

— "At the Landing"

THRUSH

Directly below Loch a spotted thrush walked noisily
in the weeds, pointing her beak ahead of her straight
as a gun, just as busy in the world as people.

— "June Recital"

STARLINGS

In the wake of their footsteps, the birds settled again.

Down on the ground, they were starlings, all on the

waddle, pushing with the yellow bills of spring.

— *The Optimist's Daughter*

PIGEONS

Moving slowly as sunlight over the grass were the broad and dusty backs of pigeons.

— "The Winds"

HERON

But before them the white heron rested in the grasses

with the evening all around it, lighter and more serene

than the evening, flight closed in its body, the circuit

of its beauty closed, a bird seen and a bird still,

its motion calm as if it were offered: Take my flight....

— "A Still Moment"

SEA GULLS

A flock of them, collected points of light halfway up
the sky, made a turn all at one time, and showed
the facets of their flight clear as a diamond.

— "Music from Spain"

QUAIL

A quail with her young walked fat as the queen
across the tangled path.

— The Robber Bridegroom

GUINEAS

Ellipses, small homebodies of great orbits

     (little knots at the back like apron strings),

Perfected, sealed off, engraved like a dozen

     perfect consciences.

          — "A Flock of Guinea Hens
             Seen from a Car"

BUZZARDS

Buzzards floated from one side of the swamp to the other, as if choice existed for them—raggedly crossing the sky and shadowing the track, and shouldering one another on the solitary limb of a moon-white sycamore.

— "Moon Lake"

CHICKENS

Beyond this was the last fence, and there the bantam

flock pecked, like one patch quilt moving with somebody

under it.

— *Losing Battles*

Cicada

CREATURES

SQUIRRELS

A pack of courting squirrels electrified a pine tree
in front of them, poured down it, ripped on through
bushes, trees, anything, tossing the branches,
sobbing and gulping like breasted doves, and
veered the other way.

— *Losing Battles*

KITTEN

Outside, she picked up a striped kitten that was stalking

through the grass-blades, and held him to her,

pressing against the tumult in her fingers and in his body.

The willful little face was like a question close to hers,

and the small stems of its breath came up and tickled

her nose like flowers.

— *Delta Wedding*

HORSE

But the horse with a wayward toss of his head

turned around in the road and trotted back down again,

his tail streaming bright as frost behind.

— Losing Battles

FIREFLIES

All around swam the fireflies. Clouds of them,

trees of them, islands of them floating,

a lower order of brightness.

— "Moon Lake"

BEES

A black funnel of bee passed through the air,

throwing a funneled shadow, like a visitor from nowhere,

another planet.

— "Moon Lake"

LOCUSTS

With a long sound like a stream of dry seed being poured
into an empty bucket, the song of the locusts began.

— *Losing Battles*

CRICKETS

The thing that seemed like silence must have been

the endless cry of all the crickets and locusts

in the world, rising and falling.

— "The Wide Net"

BUTTERFLIES

The whole world seemed filled with butterflies. At each
step they took, two black butterflies over the flowers were
whirring just alike, suspended in the air, one circling the
other rhythmically, or both moving from side to side in
a gentle wave-like way, one above the other. They were
blue-black and moving their wings faster than Jenny's eye
could follow, always together, like each other's shadows,
beautiful each one with the other. Jenny could see to
start with that no kiss had ever brought love tenderly
enough from mouth to mouth.

— "At the Landing"

MOTHS

Every girl saw moths—the beautiful ones like ladies,
with long legs that were wings—and the little ones,
mere bits of bark.

— "Moon Lake"

NIGHT INSECTS

The night insects all over the Delta were noisy,

a kind of audible twinkling, like a lowly starlight,

pervaded the night with a gregarious radiance.

— *Delta Wedding*

FROGS

Like thousands of silver bells the frogs rang her

through the swamp, which then closed behind her.

— "At the Landing"

SNAKES

All snakes, harmless and harmful, were freely playing
now; they put a trailing, moony division between
weed and weed—bright, turning, bright and turning.

— "Moon Lake"

Fall Creek

THE SEASONS

SPRING

The sky moved, soft and wet and gray, but the ground
underfoot was powder dry. Where an old sycamore
had blown over the spring before, there was turned up
a tough round wall of roots and clay all white, like the
moon on the ground. The river had not backed up
into the old backing places. Vines, leafless and yet
abundant and soft, covered the trees and thickets as if
rain clouds had been dropped down from the sky
over them. The swamp looked gray and endless as
pictures in the Bible; wherever Dewey turned,
the world held perfectly still for moments at a time—
then a heron would pump through.

                             — "Ladies in Spring'

SUMMER

At the girls' shoulders Queen Anne's lace and elderberry

and blackberry thickets, loaded heavily with flower

and fruit and smelling with the melony smell of snake,

overhung the ditch to touch them. The ditches had dried

green or blue bottoms, cracked and glazed—like a

dropped vase.

— "Moon Lake'

FALL

Each tree like a single leaf, half hair-fine skeleton,

half gauze and green, let the first suspicious wind

through its old, pressed shape, its summertime branches.

The air came smelling of what it was, the end

of September.

— "The Wanderers"

WINTER

Now, too late, when the city opened out so softly in
beauty and to such distances, it awoke a longing for
that careless, patched land of Mississippi winter,
trees in their rusty wrappers, slow-grown trees
taking their time, the lost shambles of old cane,
the winter swamp where his own twin brother,
he supposed, still hunted.

— "Music from Spain"

Fireflies

TIME OF DAY

SUNRISE

Mists, voids, patches of woods and naked clay,

flickered like live ashes, pink and blue. A mirror

that hung within the porch on the house wall began

to flicker as at the striking of kitchen matches.

Suddenly two chinaberry trees at the foot of the yard

lit up, like roosters astrut with golden tails.

— *Losing Battles*

MORNING

When they turned off, it was still early in the pink and green fields. The fumes of morning, sweet and bitter, sprang up where they walked. The insects ticked softly, their strength in reserve; butterflies chopped the air, going to the east, and the birds flew carelessly and sang by fits and starts, not the way they did in the evening in sustained and drowsy songs.

— "The Wide Net"

AFTERNOON

For that journey, it was ripe afternoon, and all about her

was that light in which the earth seems to come into

its own, as if there would be no more days,

only this day—when fields glow like deep pools and

the expanding trees at their edges seem almost to open,

like lilies, golden or dark; She had always loved

that time of day…

— "The Wanderers"

SUNSET

They had come to a great live-oak tree at the edge
of a low marshland. The burning sun hung low,
like a head lowered on folded arms, and over the long
reaches of violet trees the evening seemed still
with thought.

— "A Still Moment"

SUNSET

The sun was setting. They felt it directly behind them,
the warmth flat as a hand.

— "Moon Lake"

NIGHT

Night fell. The darkness was thin, like some sleazy dress
that has been worn and worn for many winters and
always lets the cold through to the bones.
Then the moon rose. A farm lay quite visible,
like a white stone in water, among the stretches of
deep woods in their colorless dead leaf.

— "The Whistle"

Delta Clouds

THE SKY

MOON

Under the now ash-white moon, the world traveled
through very faint stars—very many slow stars,
very high, very low.

— "No Place for You My Love"

MOON

The air wasn't darkness but faint light and floating sound.
It was the breath of all the people in the world who were
breathing out into the late night looking at the moon,
knowing her quarter.

— "The Whole World Knows"

NIGHT SKY

The night sky was pale as a green grape, transparent

like grape flesh over each tree

— "Moon Lake"

RAINBOW

But there, curved over the roof, was something he had

never seen before as long as he could remember,

a rainbow at night. In the light of the moon, which had

risen again, it looked small and of gauzy material,

like a lady's summer dress, a faint veil through which

the stars showed.

— "The Wide Net"

CLOUDS

In the sky clouds moved no more perceptibly than grazing animals.

— "Moon Lake"

CLOUDS

The sky was softly blue all over, the last rim of sunrise cloud melting into it like the foam on fresh milk.

— *Delta Wedding*

Yalobusha Swamp

PLACES

NATCHEZ TRACE

Coming upon the Trace, he looked at the high cedars, azure and still as distant smoke overhead, with their silver roots trailing down on either side like the veins of deepness in this place, and he noted some fact to his memory—this earth that wears but will not crumble or slide or turn to dust, they say it exists in one other spot in the world, Egypt—and then forgot it. He walked quietly. All life used this Trace, and he liked to see the animals move along it in direct, oblivious journeys, for they had begun it and made it, the buffalo and deer and the small running creatures before man ever knew where he wanted to go, and birds flew a great mirrored course above.

— "A Still Moment"

MISSISSIPPI RIVER

There was one hour when the river was the color of
smoke, as if it were more a thing of the woods than an
element and a power in itself. It seemed to belong to the
woods, to be gentle and watched over, a tethered and
grazing pet of the forest, and then when the light spread
higher and color stained the world, the river would leap
suddenly out of the shining ice around, into its full-grown
torrent of life, and its strength and its churning passage
held Joel watching over it like the spell unfolding by night
in his room.

— "First Love"

THE DELTA

The gold mass of the distant shade trees seemed

to dance, to sway, under the plum-colored sky. On either

side of their horses' feet the cotton twinkled like stars.

Then a red-pop flew up from her nest in the cotton.

Above in an unbroken circle, all around the wheel of the

level world, lay silvery-blue clouds whose edges

melted and changed into the pink and blue of sky.

Girls and horses lifted their heads like swimmers.

Here and there and far away the cotton wagons,

of hand-painted green, stood up to their wheel tops in

the white and were loaded with white, like cloud wagons.

— *Delta Wedding*

MOON LAKE

Luminous of course but hidden from them, Moon Lake
streamed out in the night. By moonlight sometimes
it seemed to run like a river. Beyond the cry of the frogs
there were the sounds of a boat moored somewhere,
of its vague, clumsy reaching at the shore, those sounds
that are recognized as being made by something sightless.

— "Moon Lake"

HILL COUNTRY

Here the road had all but reached its highest point.

It came winding and climbing toward them between

clay banks that reared up grooved and red as peach pits

standing on end. Little pink and yellow gravelstones,

set like the seeds in long cuts of watermelon banded

all the banks alike, running above the road—

more gravel than the road had ever received in its life.

— *Losing Battles*

Watercolors by Robin Whitfield

I choose to work out of doors; I spend many hours exploring the natural environment of Mississippi. The mysteries within the swamps, creek beds, and hardwood forests keep me exhilarated and full of questions; this, above all things, is the driving force of my painting. However, great artistic influence comes to me from two converging directions. The first is a color language used to describe light and atmosphere by working directly from nature, as taught by Sammy Britt. The second is in the creative influences coming from the spirit of the work and lives of several artists: Walter Anderson, Charles Burchfield, Emily Carr, Andy Goldsworthy, Mary Oliver, and Georgia O'Keefe. Painting feeds my curiosity, sharpens my senses, and deepens my awareness of life. I hope my work reflects a fraction of the beauty I experience.

ROBIN WHITFIELD was born and raised in Clinton, Mississippi, near Jackson, hometown of Eudora Welty. She received her BFA in painting from Delta State University in 1996, and continues to study with her professor Sammy Britt. When she is not in her outdoor studio/kayak, her work can be viewed at her downtown studio in Grenada, Mississippi, in occasional shows across the state or anytime at her online gallery, www.robinwhitfield.com.